Epps CreativeMindz Enterprise, LLC
Epps Creativemindz Publishing

ISBN-10: 0-9980567-4-X
ISBN-13: 978-0-9980567-4-6

Copyright © 2017

As Jesus comforts his disciples in John 14:1 reads, "Do not let your hearts be troubled. You believe in God; believe also in me." God's the way and the truth and the life. Our devotional offers encouragement in a biblical form and through our personal testimonies. Life is a precious gift. Through this insightful devotional, reclaim yourself, your passions, your purpose through the daily reminders of what really matters. Counting blessings of what is present and less on what is not. Embrace what really matters most, and start living life with purpose, faith, and spiritual meaning. John 3:16 For God so loved the world that he gave his one and only Son, that whoever believes in him shall not perish but have eternal life.

As you read this inspirational toolkit for your life, you will be motivated, inspired and gain the wisdom that you need to help you face and maneuver through some of those tough issues of life. Life doesn't stop because difficulties happen. Life is a precious gift. Reclaim yourself, your passions, your purpose through the daily reminders of what really matters. Counting blessings of what is present and less on what is not. Embrace what really matters most, and start living life with purpose, faith, and spiritual meaning. John 3:16 For God so loved the world that he gave his one and only Son, that whoever believes in him shall not perish but have eternal life.

James says trials will reveal whether our faith is genuine (James 1:3), and will strengthen and mature us (v. 4). The apostle Paul also believed that suffering is beneficial. He said, "we can rejoice . . . when we run into problems and trials, for we know that they help us develop endurance. And endurance develops strength of character, and character strengthens our confident hope of salvation. And this hope will not lead to disappointment" (Rom. 5:3–5 nlt). Read James 1:12 and consider what's in store for those who endure testing through faith in Jesus.

By Amy Peterson

T.G.I.F.

TODAY, GOD IS FIRST

10 *things I'm grateful for:*

1._____

2._____

3._____

4._____

5._____

6._____

7._____

8._____

9._____

10._____

What do I want to change:

_____

_____

_____

_____

3 new things to would like to try:

1._____

2._____

3._____

3 things I want to practice today:

1._____

2._____

3._____

Do you know what it means to love yourself unconditionally?

_____

_____

_____

_____

Do you know how to totally accept and embrace yourself fully?

_____

_____

_____

_____

Are you facing difficulties with loving yourself?

_____

_____

_____

_____

Just for a moment, tune in. Listen to your self-talk. Is the following self-talk true of you?

_____

_____

_____

_____

Act on what you need rather than what you want. You love yourself when you can turn away from something that feels good and exciting to what you need to stay strong, centered, and moving forward in your life, instead. By staying focused on what you need, you turn away from automatic behavior patterns that get you into trouble, keep you stuck in the past, and lessen self-love.

...And why forward is the ONLY direction!

20 Keep Moving Forward Quotes List

1. When the road gets though, don't be afraid just change your shoes

2. When you do an assessment on individuals around you and if you have a X by their name that affirmation they need to go. X means exit

3. Discover you own inner strength and take your power back and make a transformation.

4. Reaching your goals does not bring happiness, but the journey you took to get there.

5. In the mist of pain, later had something worth writing about.

6. Silence creates a self-made bomb waiting to explode.

7. With my growth came wisdom and with wisdom come understanding

8. Your situation does not determine your final destination

9. I had made many mistakes to the perfect but I have too many blessing to be ungrateful.

10. Success prompts determination and hard work

11. Success don't embrace laziness or procrastination.

12. Delegate task to others and manage time wisely

13. Don't say you can't until you have tried

14. When the Lord speaks listen attentively

15. When you find strength from God you remain faithful and loyal no matter what loss or pain you had felt.

"If you can't fly then run, if you can't run then walk, if you can't walk then crawl, but whatever you do you have to keep moving forward." ~ Martin Luther King Jr.

"Life is an ever-flowing process and somewhere on the path some unpleasant things will pop up – it might leave a scar, but then life is flowing, and like running water, when it stops it grows stale. Go bravely on, my friend, because each experience teaches us a lesson. Keep blasting because life is such that sometimes it is nice and sometimes it is not." ~ Bruce Lee

Keep Moving Forward

Exercises:

Level 1 Challenge: Make a firm commitment to yourself right now that regardless of what happens to you in life you're always going to do your best to keep moving forward. Think about the challenges and obstacles that you're facing right now and say to yourself that you will keep moving forward in spite of them. Stay strong with your will and your actions and life will follow!

_____

_____

_____

_____

_____

_____

_____

_____

_____

_____

_____

_____

_____

_____

_____

_____

_____

_____

Level 2 Challenge: Pick one quote from the collection above that stood out to you the most and tell us how that quote relates to you and your life. What you think others can learn from your unique life experience(s) in relation to it?

_____
_____
_____
_____
_____
_____
_____
_____
_____
_____
_____
_____
_____
_____
_____
_____
_____
_____
_____
_____
_____

Level 3 Challenge: Share with us a time in your life when you were able to keep moving forward in spite of a very challenging situation that you were facing. You never know who might relate to your story and find value in what you share!

_____
_____
_____
_____
_____
_____
_____
_____
_____
_____
_____
_____
_____
_____
_____
_____
_____
_____
_____
_____
_____
_____

How valuable is your life?

_____

_____

_____

_____

_____

_____

_____

_____

_____

_____

Are you willing to take the risk to rebuild?

Yes   No

Poem of Reflection

Don't Quit

When things go wrong as they often do,

And the road seems so far away,

funds are low but the debts are high

you want to smile, but you have a frown,

life is weighing you down,

You seem lost or you just don't have away.

Life is filled with twists and turns,

As we all know,

many a failure and mistakes

But life is a lesson, so learn from it;

Don't give up even when it seems you are losing the race

You may fall but only to get back up

Keep moving,

Success soon too come

Don't hide when the silver tinted clouds are near,

Stand firm and embrace it

Your faith is being tested and your break through is near

Don't quit

when things seem at its worst

Instead be victorious & courageous

Fight until the end

~ Author DuWanda S. Epps~

"FAITH
IS TAKING THE
FIRST STEP
EVEN WHEN YOU DON'T
SEE THE WHOLE
STAIRCASE."

– MARTIN LUTHER KING, JR.

Happiness keeps you smile,

Trial keeps you strong,

Tears keep you human,

Failures keeps you determined

Success keep you humble

But God keeps you going!

The most effective way
to do it,

is to do it.

-Amelia Earhart

Notes:

_____

_____

_____

_____

_____

_____

_____

_____

_____

_____

_____

_____

_____

Say Connected

Epps CreativeMindz Enterprise

Upcoming Projects & Opportunities for all seeking writer's experiences needed:
Daily Inspirational Devotion (2017)
Single Fathers Journey, I have a Heart.
Youth Creative Writing Project (2017)

Past Project:
Children's Poetry "Rhymes & Reasons (2016)- A young author entrepreneurship opportunity project

Released:
Women on a Mission
Fear to Freedom
Broken Silence: Life After the Rain (Autobiography of DuWanda S. Conway)
Unleashed Em' Shackles been Broken (Self-help, Motivation, Encouragement)
Naturally Beautiful Me
Sine me Libri Gloria
Naturellement Belle Me Activity
When I grow up
Als ich erwachsen warden
Tre'Zure Box (erotica)
Flowin Emotions
Flowin Emotions ll (Self-help books)
Emociones Flowin II: Flowin Emotions ll
Pain 2 Passion: Our Valley Experience
Chocolate & Diamonds: Celebrating the Majesty of Motherhood

Children Selections:
Anastasia Adventures

Friends & Me
Amis et moi
Amigos y Me
Hooray 4 Learning (English & Spanish Learning)
Rhymes & Reasons

<u>New Released Published</u>
Diamond Skyes Novels:
Blue Skyes
Dark Knight

<u>Just Filmed- Short Film/ Documentary:</u>

A short film about an African American woman's story of triumph, abuse, and faith. The main character witnesses' domestic violence as a child, then grows up to be in a violent relationship herself. She also experiences sexual abuse as well as being a homeless pregnant teen. Her broken marriage leads to a near drug overdose. Despite the hurt and pain, she graduated high school, college and earn a Master's Degree at the age of 25. A world of struggles did not keep her from being the woman and living the life destined for her.

Stay Tune Broken Silence: Life After the Rain
Theatrical Play
2017-18

Stay Connected:
www.flowinemotions.weebly.com
https://www.linkedin.com/in/authordsepps
authordsepps@outlook.com
Twitter: flowinemotions
Instagram: BestSellinAuthorDSE
www.eppscreativemindzenterprise.com

Epps CreativeMindz Enterprise, LLC
CreativeMindz Book Lounge
Epps CreativeMindz Publishing
Epps Tax & Notary Service
G&D Soulful Café & Lounge

Cultivating Change II, Inc
Community Outreach Project
KidzCorner

www.ingramcontent.com/pod-product-compliance
Lightning Source LLC
Chambersburg PA
CBHW051050030426
42339CB00006B/294